The Garden

poems

Marzetta

ISBN: 978-1-958859-03-2

Book design by P.D. Edgar.

Marzetta's House LLC

I had to learn
to love
myself.

Sit still
enough to hear
my own heartbeat.

Then, I was able

to tend to my own garden.

I dedicated the first edition of this book to my ex-wife…
Three years later, I return to *The Garden* to harvest and be nourished.

So, I re-dedicate this book to myself and the gays.

Foreword by the Author

The second edition of The Garden is cleaning my wounds and pruning away my past limitations. It reclaims my time, my value, my self worth, and my dedication to growing something beautiful in this lifetime. It claims renewal. A new feeling, a new life, a new format, a new release.

Welcome to The Garden.
Eden-intended and Full.

It is unapologetically Black, Southern, and Queer.

Table of Contents

WARNING

You can't come into my garden
if you don't love me.

No.
You can't pick my flowers.
No.
You can't eat my greens or
drink my wine that I
pressed from my
muscadine tears.

No.
You won't feel my grass.

And don't look over the fence either.

Now listen here...

I was born late... always took my time
        so my body can rest
             and slow down.

      So, listen here, my friend,
    Slow it all the way down.

Now, fix a cup of *tea*   cuz we're about to
go on a trip   self   exploration

      grief   recovery   healing
         growth   prosperity
           joy.

    Breathe, my friend, breathe...

     No, this ain't for everybody.
      This is for *you.*

    So, slow down and really *feel* me.

This book was written for you.
Read this leisurely.

Set you up a nice lil bougie reading nook,
take notes for the gurls in the back.

Take ownership of yourself
your power
your harvest.

Our ancestors already planted the seeds
So, reap joy everlasting
prune bitternesss and anger.

There is power in the tongue.
We are powerful.

Don't take this power lightly.

Hometown

She calls her Houston, electing
to go by her hometown rather
than a name.
It's easier that way:
naming comes with feeling
with feeling comes undoing.
She cannot afford to undo
meticulously sewn threads-
her handmedown tapestry.
Suburban comfort & expectation
stitched together since she was able to
open her mouth & told to close it.
Lesbian or lover are forbidden words
she may only read in braille
written between Houston's thighs...
Houston is like bubblegum sherbet: an
idea a child would find delightful-
an adult disturbing.

Yet, she allows herself the moment to indulge
sapping up sweet syrup
just before it hits the ground.

She briefly lets her mind wonder
what would happen
if they knew.

She smirks into Houston's neck,
offering hers in return,
tracing intricate patterns of maybe
chest to chest.

Sepia meets hickory,
sticky with love dew-
p r o m i s e s
they don't bother to make
out loud.

She allows herself to be kissed
& enjoys the taste of bubblegum.

The Hike

Three college graduates go for a hike:
two girls, one guy.
One of the girls needs to use the restroom.
The college students drive around
a foreign neighborhood
composed of mountains and American flags.
A man watering his grass looks into the car
smiles, tight-lipped and reserved;
there are no colleges on this side of town.
No niggas either.

Three niggas go for a hike:
two girls, one guy.
They drive around and find a park.
The air sings bicycle bells and baseball snuff—
as American as any Alabama suburb can be.
By the park restrooms are City workers
resting in their truck on a bed of mud and concrete.
Clipped trees offer them shade
They give blueberry juul smoke in return.
One girl gets out the car. The other girl stays.
She looks at the guy in his pink-pandemic mask.
She tells him to stay in the car.

Three niggas go for a hike:
two girls, one fag.
The girls get out the car, leaving the air on for the
faggot to breathe in mid-May heat. They walk in
survival-position towards rusty doors and the
integrated water hole.
The door is locked.
One girl sighs in disappointment,
the Other watches the men
who look over at the clang of a stubborn industrial lock
against the will of a nigga-gal's bladder.
The truck full of white men drives away.
The Black men stay.

Unnamed Suga or Sweet Thang, the girls breathe relief.
Black Man #1 hands a sista the keys.
The Other wonders what if
their companion had gotten out of the car...
if Black Man #2 would have seen a brotha or sissy and
followed the faggot into the men's room,
curious if he takes a piss in the bowl or on the floor.
She looks in the mirror and shakes her head clear,
comforted with soft affirmations of womanhood— a
chameleon of Southern-Belle, product of Blue Magic.

Satisfied with her ability to pass,
they walk out the restroom,
dropping clunky keys in calloused hands.
There would be no lynching today.
No niggas under a citizen's arrests of Klan and kill;
no fag turned to fig; no Baartman exhibition; no
examination of the bestial blend, one-part woman,
equal parts dyke.

Three niggas go for a hike:
one girl, one fag, one dyke.
If they make it to their destination,
they will decide which one wins.

Busy Bee Buzz

[Dull. Stuck. Aware. Absent. Here.]

[*Tick. Tock. Tick. Tock. click clack. click clack. click clack.*] *"Hey, bud. Do me a favor?"* [*RING! RING!*] *"Hello?" "Bob, you got those reports yet?"* [*click clack. click clack. click clack.*] *"Greta! Nice to see you, girl! How's the wife?"* [*tap tap tap tap tap tap tap tap*] *"I'm sorry. It just won't work. Try again next time." "Maybe we'll have the money by then.."* [*tap tap tap tap tap tap tap tap tap*] *"Anyway, Bob, whatcha think about this?"* [*RING! RING!*] *"You've got Sue. What can I do for you?"* click clack. click clack. click clack. *"Hi, Sue. I am missing-"* [*RING! RING!*] *"WHERE ARE THOSE GODDAMNED REPORTS?!"* [*tap tap tap tap tap tap tap tap*]

ENOUGH!

Air.

I need air.

Check point

Hey girl,
Take a moment.
Breathe...
Stop thinking so much.
Clear your mind
Clear your heart.
Do you feel that?
The breath in your lungs?
The air hitting your insides?
Relax your shoulders then
take a deep breath.
Let it all in,
Let it all out.
You know what that is?
That's peace.
That's intention.
That's power.
That's God.
Breathe, baby.
You will be okay.

God's got you.
Breathe...
and breathe again.
One more time.
Alright, now.
You got this.

& They all sing:

take one step to the river
then take two
hands raised in the Garden
you know what to do.

daughter, you are made of bone & clay
will of Ancestor/ water of womb//

walk gently into the river
hold hand of breeze & intention/
sink soundly
& wash your feet/
feel
steady ripples
salt & affirmation//

daughter, go gently
into the river
you in God's hands now/
ain't it good?
don't it feel nice?

to be held at the bosom
of Sheba & Mary//

allow these truths:
let go.
be loved/
cry
(loud/
softly).

daughter, fall gently into the river
you in God's hands now/
aint it good? don't it feel nice?
to be held at Mother's bosom &
baptized by Son.

THE GARDEN

this body is made for movement
song and dance work and
sweat/ pick and sift red clay and
stone till the soil 'til brown beds
raise themselves

into a home of sweet peas and
squash/ cabbages the children will
not eat, tomatoes to be fried green or
stewed with the mucilage of okra/

this body was made to tend to the garden
with firm hands just gentle enough to
snap purple hulls and avoid worms, pick
trees of fig and plum-plump and juicy like
the hips gifted to me by big mama and
cornbread/

grape veins etched into pecan skin make
themselves known as the soil is worked, grass
parted like tender-headed plats done on the
front porch between grit-creased knees risen
from earth and alter/ rainwater and raised
beds are to canned grease and scalp/ there is
a healing after the fire and the beans begin to
sprout as babies learn mama from milk/

come to the garden
and see for yourself
movement/
growth/ The One.

Grounded

I would like to blame COVID
but it was a way   out.

         I hadn't been to church in 3 years.
    1095 days 56 Sundays 36 communions 21 vacation
            bible school lessens
                Missed.

I missed them.
      But I liked my freedom better.

I liked living room prayers on Facebook live,
Shot glass communion   drink the blood of merlot
Broke the body of hot Cheetos & oatmeal cream pies

           I called on

Yahweh   Ancestor   Tarot   El Shaddai
         & my best bitches!

        I been prayin on Bourbon Street

High as fuck   screaming   crying
"THANK YOU, GAWD!"
Watch the magic   mic drop of queer gurls in leather
Shout, "JEEZUS!" in a poetry slam--

I ain't been to church but I found a healing
Deep down on the Inside
Attend the bonfire in my bones
infuse my soul with mac n cheese & $10 tree
Roll down the palm leaves
swifter than a Swisher goes
Missing
Pocket benediction cuz GAWD ain't goin nowhere-
I   ain't goin   nowhere.

I
am.
Here. Saved. Queer. Loved.
Happy.
Whole.
I
am.

I got married despite being unable to be married by my
pastors   who helped me
shoot myself from the pews
cuz being accepting is cool but doing the work is Hell.
I ain't get married in a church,
BUT GAWD!   Spirit   was moving
Grandmas   praying
Daddies dancing
Mamas   grinning   giggling
cuz their babies
made it!
Cuz we knew God for ourselves
&   finally   saw
Heaven.

The ground must be burned
to harvest the new crop

When the fire begins to burn,
the Farmers cover their eyes.
Flames make a deal with the sun,
meeting its heat with their own.

The Farmers get on their knees to pray,
run soil between printless fingers,
watch the dirt crumble
as the ashes rise...
cling to all that is present.

Soil:
the farmer thinks,
Particles of dust in remembrance of what it once was.

Peace
that flows

is Still

is Patience

is Mercy

is Grace

is Love

is Kindness

is Joy

is Feeling

all the Things

that make us Human

is Knowing

that God

is still God

releasing it All

embracing the Moment

for what It Is

accepting that It Will Be

Okay.

You   are   okay.

Check point

Hey, sweet girl.
Breathe.
Let it all in...
Let it all out.

U-Haul Love Bomb

After eating bomb ass phillys on her bed stuffed with
too many blankets, I asked if I could use some
mouthwash. She said *yes* and causally inserted that I
should have brought a toothbrush . I laughed because I
literally just met her a week ago. But, damn, if the lovin
didn't feel good. Damn if her arms didn't feel like the
right amount of comfort and the right amount of home
when home was 200 miles away, wrapped in blue
masks. I looked over at her smile that gleamed joy and
acceptance. She didn't know that it was the first smile
unhidden by a mask I've been able to see in months;
that the last time I was in the arms of someone I loved,
it was only for a second in fear of getting COVID; that
high risk in a pandemic means high risk for loneliness.
She doesn't know I didn't see my grandmother's smile
as much as I wanted; that instead of reading her lips I
had to rely on eyes to cut in whatever direction (like
she used to do in church) to understand...

I didn't hug anyone last time I went home; I didn't get to kiss my mom on the cheek or make sure that she closed it out by kissing mine in return; my dad didn't get to see my first apartment; I didn't get to see Mrs. Alphonsia's smile before ___ ; she didn't get to see our smiles the last time as she wondered what was on our faces, a foreign protection that broke us into fragments...

So, when my lover told me to bring a toothbrush, she didn't know she was telling me to come home.

Bad Bitch in Snake Skins

She reeks of power
Struts and poses
She is *that bitch* and you know it
She is unbothered
She is confident
She is limitless
She is *that bitch* and you know it

after the storm

the river is too high and no longer beautiful

-at least the kind of
beautiful i like.

the water is brown-- a dirty brown
warped and uneasy:
ugly.
no longer clear and sky blue,
swamp-like waves slash through one another,
while the water tries to find a way
back
to itself.
and the trees-
the last of the Pocahontas trees-
gloriously cracked sticks made of too
many splits and rough-mahogany craters for
memory-
stand tall and proud
like they ought to be the center of attention
just because they survived
the storm

(and all the others too).

big, wide, flat leaves- so perfect and deep bright green
look like they ought to taste of min tastes like dirt;
probably that very dirt that turned the water so sour
and the bank too disturbing to stomach for too long.

The sky is pretty, though… not a
trace of ash-grey disruption or
sponge-soaked clouds; just blue-

still

a truly beautiful blue.
you'd never know
how the sky opened its mouth, spat on us so
hard and nasty,
swallowed up nine people just last night.
i guess that's why they tell you
look up not down.

Pruning

[daughter's teen years are whispered giggles and
late-night phone calls
mama's eyes flash warningly when they see the call]
log mama says who is she
[daughter doesn't answer]
mama says is she your girlfriend
daughter says she just a friend from school
[mama gives the phone back
daughter doesn't mention that the school is not hers]

mama says college is different
daughter says she's glad
mama   says   graduate
with a ring daughter says maybe
mama says I want a son-in-law
daughter says maybe one day
mama says not a daughter-in-law

[daughter freezes]
mama says where's your boyfriend
daughter says she's focusing on school
mama says fix your makeup and look nice
daughter says her skin is too sensitive

mama says why don't you wear lipstick

daughter says she doesn't need to wear it all the time

mama says you look too masculine   daughter

says she can't help her face mama   says why

are you being mannish daughter says not

intentionally mama says she hates the new profile

picture daughter says she loves it mama   says be

who you aren't just a little while longer daughter

says she can't mama   says please

daughter says okay mama   says thank you

daughter says mhm

mama says please find a husband   daughter

          says she can't   mama

says she won't

love   unnatural grandkids daughter

          says she can't

have kids anyway   mama

          says daughter

                              is her curse

[daughter feels her heart break]

mama says she's sorry
daughter says mhm
mama says please stay daughter
says i can't   mama
says come home   daughter
says make it safe   mama
says mhm
daughter says please   mama
says i can't
daughter
says the world ain't safe
either
mama says she knows daughter
says she's sorry
mama says forgiveness daughter
says acceptance.
[End Act One]

There is a woman in the shadows

Waiting to be free
Skin of wood and will of iron
She looks just like me

There is a woman in the shadows
Waiting to be free
Voice soft as angels
Sing this sweet melody

Of courage and wisdom
Beauty and pain
Of ash and sycamore
Strength and gain

There is a woman in the shadows
She looks just like me
Eyes elusive
Body waiting
For her moment to be free.

On the days that feel like soup|

|and look like sorbet

grab a spoon
& choose which one to indulge.

my side of town

At the light on the corner of Title Max in the
Neighborhood Walmart, it's the battle of the bass. Let's
see whose stereo spits the loudest beats, makes ya face
say '*Oooh shit! That's Nasty,*' just like that hole in the
wall down the street: barely changes the gloves
between making food and taking orders but it's that
extra spice of dirt that makes the best jerk; it's the fried
fish plate for $5 down at the church for Bebe's college
fund; for Pookie's jail bond; or Nina's babie; it's the
shower at the Community Center that's the highlight of
the month for some folks-- the day for others.

On my side, you have Wing Stop and the Chicken Box;
on the Other Side, you have Chicken Salad Chick and
Nothing Bundt Cakes, not the butter loaf birthday cake
from Miss Emma's apartment. When Mom took me
over to the pink-tinged complex on my 13th birthday, I
wondered where the frosting was. At age 20, all it took
was a 15 minute drive to find out the icing on the cake
is on the South side— that Whole Foods had queen-
wah; that their movie theater had free refills on slushies
rather than having to wait to pass Chevron. I started
taking that 15-minute drive once a week introducing my
friends to a side of town they didn't know existed. But
after getting pulled over by blue lights, that shit ain't
worth the hype. So, I'm back on my side now; safe and
sound. I love it here.

Walking into womanhood on a undefined nose bridge

Keep your head up, chile, it's a long road ahead.

We Still Livin'

Karaoke with the gurls
& Henny margaritas
turn to Sunday yoga
& prayer at a poetry slam.
27 might not be so bad after all.

The White Gays at the Farmer's Market

[actors may be the stereotype of your choice]

Gay No. 1:

Mmm, mmm, mmm! This kambucha queen-wah wine
is delicious! Gurl, where did you find this?!

Gay No. 2:

Honey, just over there.

Saw him werking away selling his stuff by the kale,

I said *yasss, girl!*

I walked up to him and said

Let me give it to you, boo!

Now, he looked surprised

but I just smiled into his big brown eyes

and he grinned back at me

so charming, I thought I was Diana, bitch!

I said *yasss, girl!*

I knew I had him trapped by the cookie!

He changed my world.

Gave me a baby *three* times as many grapes I got

I said yasss, girl!

Werked it til he ran out of grapes!

When a Black Gurl Lives Joy

" P   E   R   I   O   D   D   D   D   D   !   !   !   "
says the fine ass   Black   g   u   r   l
crop top   blonde   booty-length   braids
     Grin   on   ten
Mustache   connected   to   beard
     eyebrows ain't the only thang arched tonite!
Black   gurl   says,
" A   L   R   I   G   H   T   ,   N   O   W   !   "
She   sashays   away-
Spins,   hips   dips,
Stands   pop,   POPS!
S   H   A   K   E   S   S   S
Those   musical   legs
Wrapped   in   leather.
  True Gemini-coy (bitten lips and fluttered lash),
the   Belly Laugh   announces   their   presence
and   shakes   hands   with   Spirit.
Black   gurl   looks   *gooood,*
Feels   damn   good,   too!

-For Our Trans Sisters: Our history will not be erased.

say It with me

I am

unstoppable

I am

Godly

I am

THAT

I am

powerful

hear me roar

and weep in victory

I have won.

I am free

to be

Me.

Thank you for reading!

Today feels like plum wine and hope.

Acknowledgments

Thank you to the village who helped raise my garden.

This book was written in honor of the poetry that saved my life. Without those words, I would not have held on to the hope and faith that led me to love and live life fully and authentically.

To the Black queer youths in the Piggly Wiggly, hiding in the riverbed and in the fields, or stuffing the evidence of yourself into the bottom of a book bag:

I see you; I hear you; I feel you... I hope that after reading this, you see you, too. I hope you imagine that love you want, and live your best dream come true.

Tend to your garden; reap joy abundantly and limitless imagination.

About the Author

Kaitlyn Marzetta McClung is an Austin-based multidisciplinary artist, musician, and literary scholar. Rooted in Black Southern queerness and womanhood, Marzetta's work bridges creativity and academia.

Marzetta was named a 2024 emerging artist by the Utah Literary Arts Festival. A published poet and essayist, Marzetta has performed at the New York City Poetry Festival, Deep Vellum Books in Dallas, and bookstores across the United States. Marzetta is open for bookings at venues and universities around the globe.